The Miracle Working God

Lawson Hanson

Dedication

To Almighty God, The Creator, Who cares for us and heals us, and fills us with His precious Holy Spirit. He provides us with the wonderful fruit of: Love, Joy, Peace, Longsuffering, Gentleness, Goodness, Faith, Meekness and Temperance. To the one and only, true miracle-working God.

See: Galatians 5:22,23.

Contents

Chapter 1

Beginnings

Wonderful aspects of certainty and tangible evidential experiences got incorporated into my life as I migrated from my doubtful beginnings of uncertain belief in God through to a position where I enjoy having an absolute assurance of the faith that is given to believers in Almighty God and His righteous Son Jesus Christ.

I consider myself a *"born again"* Christian.

What does that mean?

The gospel of John chapter 3 reports an instance when Jesus speaks to a man named Nicodemus who was a Pharisee and a ruler of the Jews:

> 1. *There was a man of the Pharisees, named Nicodemus, a ruler of the Jews:*
> 2. *The same came to Jesus by night, and said unto him, Rabbi, we know that thou art a teacher come from God: for no man can do these miracles that thou doest, except God be with him.*
> 3. *Jesus answered and said unto him, Verily, verily, I say unto thee, Except a man be born again, he cannot see the kingdom of God.*

4. Nicodemus saith unto him, How can a man be born when he is old? can he enter the second time into his mother's womb, and be born?
5. Jesus answered, Verily, verily, I say unto thee, Except a man be born of water and of the Spirit, he cannot enter into the kingdom of God.
6. That which is born of the flesh is flesh; and that which is born of the Spirit is spirit.
7. Marvel not that I said unto thee, Ye must be born again.
— John 3:1–7

Notice that Jesus uses the terms *"born again"* and *"born of water and of the Spirit"* and makes the emphatic statement *"Ye must be born again."*

At the time Nicodemus did not comprehend what Jesus said.

Jesus went about preaching the gospel, healing the sick and working diverse miracles among the people.

When Jesus suffered unimaginable and awful torment at the hands of the chief priests of the temple and the Roman soldiers to whom they delivered Him for trial insisting that He get taken to die on the cross:

6. When the chief priests therefore and officers saw him, they cried out, saying, Crucify him, crucify him. Pilate saith unto them, Take ye him, and crucify him: for I find no fault in him.
7. The Jews answered him, We have a law, and by our law he ought to die, because he made himself the Son of God.
— John 19:6–7

Jesus died for us:

28. *After this, Jesus knowing that all things were now accomplished, that the scripture might be fulfilled, saith, I thirst.*

29. *Now there was set a vessel full of vinegar: and they filled a spunge with vinegar, and put it upon hyssop, and put it to his mouth.*

30. When Jesus therefore had received the vinegar, he said, It is finished: and he bowed his head, and gave up the ghost.

— John 19:28–30

Joseph of Arimathaea and Nicodemus came to bury Jesus:

38. *And after this Joseph of Arimathaea, being a disciple of Jesus, but secretly for fear of the Jews, besought Pilate that he might take away the body of Jesus: and Pilate gave him leave. He came therefore, and took the body of Jesus.*

39. *And there came also Nicodemus, which at the first came to Jesus by night, and brought a mixture of myrrh and aloes, about an hundred pound weight.*

40. *Then took they the body of Jesus, and wound it in linen clothes with the spices, as the manner of the Jews is to bury.*

41. *Now in the place where he was crucified there was a garden; and in the garden a new sepulchre, wherein was never man yet laid.*

42. *There laid they Jesus therefore because of the Jews' preparation day; for the sepulchre was nigh at hand.*

— John 19:38–42

After three days Jesus arose from the dead and He spoke to His apostles and disciples for forty days and He gave them more information about this miracle coming from God:

3. *To whom also he shewed himself alive after his passion by many infallible proofs, being seen of them forty days, and speaking of the things pertaining to the kingdom of God:*
4. *And, being assembled together with them, commanded them that they should not depart from Jerusalem, but wait for the promise of the Father, which, saith he, ye have heard of me.*
5. *For John truly baptized with water; but ye shall be baptized with the Holy Ghost not many days hence.*
— Acts 1:3–5

The apostles and disciples were obedient people who waited as Jesus commanded. In the next chapter of Acts we read:

1. *And when the day of Pentecost was fully come, they were all with one accord in one place.*
2. *And suddenly there came a sound from heaven as of a rushing mighty wind, and it filled all the house where they were sitting.*
3. *And there appeared unto them cloven tongues like as of fire, and it sat upon each of them.*
4. *And they were all filled with the Holy Ghost, and began to speak with other tongues, as the Spirit gave them utterance.*
— Acts 2:1–4

This is what Jesus meant when He said:

"Ye must be born again."

Like those believers — we must get *"filled with the Holy Ghost"* and we will also begin to *"speak with other tongues"* as the Spirit gives us the utterance.

4

This identical experience has happened to me and to *all* of the members of the church that I attend.

This church had its origins in 1946 commencing here in Melbourne, Australia. It now has centres located across Australia and around the world in New Zealand, Fiji, Papua New Guinea, England, Poland, Italy, Canada, the U.S.A. and in Kenya, Tanzania and Malawi in Africa and more — thousands and thousands of *"born again"* people.

You can find out more details at its Internet link:

```
https://www.revivalcentres.org
```

In other sections below there is a brief outline of youthful days when I struggled with my believing before I heard the full gospel message presented to me by a faithful witness — a person with first hand experience of this miracle from God.

I provide some detail of the way in which we learn to walk in the newness of our Spirit-filled *"born again"* life.

Romans chapter 6 tells us this:

> 3. *Know ye not, that so many of us as were baptized into Jesus Christ were baptized into his death?*
> 4. *Therefore we are buried with him by baptism into death: that like as Christ was raised up from the dead by the glory of the Father, even so we also should walk in newness of life.*
> — Romans 6:3–4

Life is not always easy. We have ups and downs like everyone.

I will highlight events through which we (my wife and I) have needed to trust and rely upon the wonderful promises of care and provision that the Bible contains — that *"Book of books"* we both believe to be the inspired Word of God.

If you glean anything from what you read here — please understand that God has proven Himself most gracious and that He does, time and again, heal us and provide for our every need.

We need to take responsibility for what we do. We need to ensure that we are not careless as we go about taking actions which could be detrimental to health or well-being or survival.

For example, if we always drove our motor car at full speed everywhere we went then we could expect to have more — *"accidents"* — one of which could be fatal to us — or worse — to other innocent people.

We drive at or under the speed limits and take every precaution we can.

If we will not take a reasonable amount of care then we should expect we could encounter difficulties.

Personal struggles have resulted from my own lack of attention to important details that can help us to live a better and more healthy life.

I consumed a diet which included an over supply of refined sugar for years or decades with the result that I developed diabetes type 2.

I mismanaged the medications provided to me for that.

Worse, I kept drinking gallons of sweetened and caffeinated soft drinks and eating sweets and cakes and chocolates behind my own back.

I kept on gaining excessive weight. This combined with elevated levels of circulating blood glucose caused me to experience an Ischaemic stroke episode and later I needed a triple by-pass operation on my heart.

God will help us when we call upon Him and pray to Him as we have needed to do on any number of occasions.

Living and survival can get complex. There is no sense in making life more difficult than it needs to be.

God takes no particular pleasure in our stupidities.

God created us with a collection of highly refined senses to help us observe — see, hear, taste, smell, feel and ability to navigate our way through the environment.

God created us with an intelligent brain to help us process those different stimuli and has enabled us to think in great detail about everything we do. We have no excuse.

Even after we have followed God's commands and we smarten up our lives to believe what God says and we pray to Him humbly every day, events can still at times go awry.

Life continues to happen around us and to us and we can still find ourselves going through some awkward moments.

We hold fast to the faith God has bestowed upon us:

> 8. *For by grace are ye saved through faith; and that not of yourselves: it is the gift of God:*
> 9. *Not of works, lest any man should boast.*
> — Ephesians 2:8–9

We remember passages of scripture like this:

> 28. *And we know that all things work together for good to them that love God, to them who are the called according to his purpose.*
> — Romans 8:28

Incredible promises like this:

13. *There hath no temptation taken you but such as is common to man: but God is faithful, who will not suffer you to be tempted above that ye are able; but will with the temptation also make a way to escape, that ye may be able to bear it.*
— 1 Corinthians 10:13

Knowing that we have an advocate, Jesus Christ, through the infilling Holy Spirit is wonderful:

1. *My little children, these things write I unto you, that ye sin not. And if any man sin, we have an advocate with the Father, Jesus Christ the righteous:*
2. *And he is the propitiation for our sins: and not for our's only, but also for the sins of the whole world.*
— 1 John 2:1–2

Our prayers and petitions come with speed before the grace of our God. He hears and He answers our call, miraculously, as the one true God can.

I love the words in this verse from the book of Hebrews:

16. *Let us therefore come boldly unto the throne of grace, that we may obtain mercy, and find grace to help in time of need.*
— Hebrews 4:16

God knows full well that we struggle at times and His ears are always open to hear us when we remember to be humble and call out to Him.

Chapter 2

Awakening

The very first inklings of my belief in God stem from an up-bringing in a nominal *"Christian'* family where both of my parents firmly professed to believe in a higher power they called *"God."*

As a young child I spent two or three years attending a *"Church of England"* school called *"Saint Barnabas"* in Oxford, England.

We attended regular services in the Saint Barnabas church building located a short distance down Cardigan Street near where we went to school, not far from the Oxford University Press.

I used to sing in the choir and would spend one or two hours each week going to choir practise sessions at the church or in a nearby building.

I did not have any real appreciation of God in those youthful days and when I reached the tender age of ten (10) years my parents migrated, by steam ship, from Britain to Australia and my choral singing days came to an end.

The primary and secondary schools I attended in the beach suburbs of Largs Bay and Semaphore (West of Adelaide, in

South Australia) included weekly *"Religious Instruction"* classes.

At about the age of twelve (12) or thirteen (13) I first sat up to take notice and began to comprehend the greatness of God.

During my first or second year at high school we had a wonderful Religious Instruction teacher, a dear lady, who on a regular basis would read beautiful Bible stories to her class of attentive students. This is where I began to hear about the reports of the wonderful miracles performed by Jesus Christ.

We got told stories of how Jesus healed all those who came to Him. The lepers got cleansed, the deaf began to hear, the lame got given strength and ability to walk and the eyesight of the blind got restored.

Jesus even raised people (like Lazarus) from the dead. I got great comfort from the thought that our wonderful R.I. teacher believed every word she was reading to her listeners. I remember hearing this passage:

> 20. *When the men were come unto him, they said, John Baptist hath sent us unto thee, saying, Art thou he that should come? or look we for another?*
> 21. *And in that same hour he cured many of their infirmities and plagues, and of evil spirits; and unto many that were blind he gave sight.*
> 22. *Then Jesus answering said unto them, Go your way, and tell John what things ye have seen and heard; how that the blind see, the lame walk, the lepers are cleansed, the deaf hear, the dead are raised, to the poor the gospel is preached.*
> — Luke 7:20–22

The following year we had a change of R.I. teacher, a younger man, and when I got around to asking *"Where are the mir-*

acles today?" he said *"Those miracles happened when Jesus walked the earth!"* *"They do not happen now."*

I recall how dejected his off-hand statements made me feel and how I then drifted away from religion and did my own thing for the next decade!

Like most of my peers at the age of 25 years, I was drinking like an alcoholic, foul mouthed, swearing, dabbling in drugs, chain-smoking more than 30 cigarettes each day, and I had decided that everything must have happened through an inexplicable *"Cosmic Accident"*.

In the last week of January 1975, I was out of work and had started to apply for suitable employment. Soon I made it to interview stage, but I missed out on getting selected to fill a vacancy for an Electronics Technician position at the Physics Department of the University of Melbourne.

I expect I *was* attempting to bat above my average.

The following Friday night there was a party at a large house where I was renting a room. I think I smoked some marijuana which got contaminated with a residue of insecticide because I had an awful reaction to it.

I became unwell that night. I was sweating profusely with my heart beat racing. I reached a point where I thought I was going to die.

At that time I called out to God and begged *"If you are there God, please don't let me die."* At some stage I passed out and I remember nothing until late the next day.

Soon an unusual event happened.

First thing on the following Monday morning a telegram addressed to me got delivered. I think it got sent on the Friday — before I called out to God.

It came from the Department of Civil Engineering at the

University of Melbourne and it offered me a position as an Electronics Technician in their department.

They had heard that I missed out on the position at the Department of Physics and they were looking for somebody with similar skills. I attended another interview and got offered their technical position which I was glad to accept.

This was an extraordinary turn of events that I did not begin to realise and appreciate until years later.

Chapter 3

A Faithful Testimony

A week or so after I had commenced working at my new place of employment, Martin, a Ph.D. student, returned from semester break to resume his project work. He began to tell me, and the other people there, about the solid belief he had in the God of the Bible.

He declared in his faithful testimony to us that his God was still performing miracles of provision and healing for His believing people today. This immediately sounded like music to my ears.

About five months later — I was a bit slow — I was greatly encouraged and convinced to attend a Revival Centres church meeting. Here is that link again:

```
https://www.revivalcentres.org
```

The moment I walked through the doors I felt as if I had "*come home.*" I was thoroughly impressed by the great sea of the smiling faces.

They were a vibrant mix with people of all ages — young, middle-aged and the more elderly. Remarkable to me, I noticed, they conversed with each other — no age barriers.

Listening to the Bible talks that day I heard the same message the Ph.D. student had been trying to tell me for months.

Martin was well versed with his Bible and turned to each new passage as the speaker announced from where he was about to read.

I was able to follow along and could read — there on the pages in black-and-white — that if I would obey God's commandments to repent and get baptized by full immersion — submerged in water — then I could expect that God would respond to me, personally, by filling me with His gift of the Holy Spirit.

About the act of baptism, the Bible declares:

> 21. *The like figure whereunto even baptism doth also now save us (not the putting away of the filth of the flesh, but the answer of a good conscience toward God,) by the resurrection of Jesus Christ:*
> — 1 Peter 3:21

That is — when we get baptised in this way — it demonstrates that we have *"a good conscience toward God"* showing that we are making an honest and humble approach with a contrite heart and repentant attitude toward Him.

It got explained that the word *"repent"* got translated from the Greek word *"metanoeo."*

According to two concordance references that I have examined, this word more nearly means: *"to think differently"* or *"to have another mind"* or to prayerfully *"reconsider."*

The following Sunday, after having thought all week about what I had heard I did get baptized in water and it felt wonderful. It made sense. It's not a difficult action to take.

I knew within myself that I had taken a step in the right direction — towards God instead of wandering further away from Him — as I had for a long time.

That was 22–June–1975.

It took five more weeks before I actually received the gift of the Holy Spirit.

It took me those five weeks to sort out my thinking and to understand what my repentance meant. It needed a complete change of comprehension.

On Sunday morning 27–July–1975 I was praying to God, saying *"Hallelujah"* as we get encouraged to do.

I was thinking about some of the wonderful miracles God had already done in my life.

After a while I realised I was speaking in other tongues — it felt refreshing and peaceful.

I was speaking fluently in what sounded like the words of another language — one I had never learned.

I speak English and have never learned any other.

The words came flowing out of my mouth at my normal volume and speed of speech — there is no need to shout and no unusual effort required.

The experience was most comforting.

I was in complete control of when I opened my mouth and when I chose to close it again.

I could speak in other tongues, or I could speak my natural language. The choice was mine to make.

What a wonderful personal gift God bestows upon us. Consider the following verse from 1st Corinthians, chapter 14:

> 2. *For he that speaketh in an unknown tongue*
> *speaketh not unto men, but unto God: for no*
> *man understandeth him; howbeit in the spirit he*

speaketh mysteries.
— 1 Corinthians 14:2

God provides us with precisely the words we need to say to enable us to speak directly to Him. The words enable us to worship God in the way we must:

24. *God is a Spirit: and they that worship him must worship him in spirit and in truth.*
— John 4:24

The ability to speak in an unknown tongue helps us to communicate and say what is on our mind, without us needing to stumble around to find our own words to express our innermost feelings.

This is a beautiful example of the boundless grace of God.

Chapter 4

Personal Miracles

The things about which I had been thinking, moments before I realised that I was speaking in other tongues, were the wonderful miracles which had already taken place in my life in the short space of five weeks from the time at which I got baptized.

One night I attended a smaller "*house meeting*" where I heard "*God is a healing God.*"

At the end of that meeting I asked for prayer that God would heal my nose. It had been in pain for about a year or more after I got punched in the face during a bit of a fight.

The person who prayed for me said this: "*Thank you God for healing this man's nose.*" Soon after that I went home.

During the night I woke up feeling rather warm. There was also a tingling sensation in the middle of my face — it felt as if my nose was getting a gentle manipulation around and around in a tiny circular motion.

I got up to check that there was nobody there. There wasn't — I lived alone. I soon cooled down and went back to sleep.

In the morning there was another strange sensation.

No more pain! Wow. That worked fast. Hallelujah.

At another house meeting I heard *"God can do anything!"*

I took it upon myself to say to God *"Okay God. If you can do anything: Stop me from smoking."*

Later that night, after I got home from the meeting, I went to light up a cigarette before heading off to bed. The cigarette tasted awful — foul.

I opened a new carton of cigarettes, took out a fresh pack and lit up another cigarette, discovering that the new one tasted awful, too.

In disgust (almost), I went to bed and slept soundly until the next morning. When I awoke, again I tried to light up another cigarette. This also tasted disgusting!

Since that day (about 50 years ago) I have never ever had the craving for another cigarette, in fact even the slightest smell of cigarette smoke makes me feel unwell. It reminds me to say *"Thank you Lord."*

God enabled me to quit smoking — overnight.

If you have ever been a smoker you will understand how difficult is the task of giving up that addiction to nicotine. I had tried quitting a lot of times before and had always failed within a one or two days at most.

One day during those first five weeks, the desire to drink alcohol deserted me.

I had the sudden urge to pour my small collection of wines and spirits down the sink. I did that. It felt liberating.

Since doing that I have never wanted to touch another glass of beer or wine or alcohol of any kind.

Another thing I noticed is my speech was beginning to contain less and less profanities and expletives.

Those miracles astounded me and the fact that my senses of taste and smell were starting to return.

I realised I was sleeping soundly every night instead of tossing and turning half awake for hours on end as I had been before I started praying to God.

When I was thinking about those wonderful miracles that God had already performed for me I gradually realised I had actually received the gift of the Holy Spirit because I was speaking in other tongues.

It felt wonderful and I kept praying for a little while, listening to those new unknown words.

That was 27-July-1975.

Over all the intervening years, since that time, the indwelling presence of God's Holy Spirit has never left me.

I have come to realise that God is both alive and well and in my estimation He has been forever.

My former appreciation of Him was at gross fault.

If we will obey God's simple commandments, like I did, I believe He will reveal Himself to us in a wonderful personal way, even as He has done so for me.

In the Book of Acts, chapter 2, verse 37, when the people asked: *"What shall we do?"* the apostle Peter's reply was this:

> 38. *Repent, and be baptized every one of you in the name of Jesus Christ for the remission of sins, and ye shall receive the gift of the Holy Ghost.*
> — Acts 2:38

We take two steps and God provides the third.

Repent — get prepared to have a change in the way we have been thinking about God. Most of us do not have a clue.

Get baptized — by full immersion under the water.

Talk to God. Call out to him in a calm and circumspect manner.

Ask Him for the gift He says He has waiting for you.

There's no need to shout. God is not deaf.

He knows our thoughts before we speak:

> 11. *The LORD knoweth the thoughts of man, that they are vanity.*
> — Psalms 94:11

Before long there will be a miraculous result when you receive the gift of the Holy Ghost and you begin to speak in other (unlearned) tongues.

I had another wonderful realisation when I received this tangible and personal proof from God.

Everything the Bible believing lady teacher at my secondary school taught me was correct in every exciting detail.

The second male teacher did not know the truth.

Miracles still *do* happen today. God never changes.

The Old Testament declares this:

> 6. *For I am the LORD, I change not; therefore ye sons of Jacob are not consumed.*
> 7. *Even from the days of your fathers ye are gone away from mine ordinances, and have not kept them. Return unto me, and I will return unto you, saith the LORD of hosts. But ye said, Wherein shall we return?*
> — Malachi 3:6, 7

The New Testament declares:

8. *Jesus Christ the same yesterday, and to day,
and for ever.*
— Hebrews 13:8

Soon after the day of Pentecost experience described in Acts chapter 2, the Holy Spirit got poured out more widely to the so called *"Gentile"* nations.

At first the Jews or Israelite believers thought this was their exclusive privilege.

The plan of God — we read — has a far wider range of ideas.

Look at these verses from the prophet Joel:

28. *And it shall come to pass afterward, that I
will pour out my spirit upon all flesh; and your
sons and your daughters shall prophesy, your old
men shall dream dreams, your young men shall
see visions:*
29. *And also upon the servants and upon the
handmaids in those days will I pour out my spirit.*
— Joel 2:28–29

"I will pour out my spirit upon all flesh" means this personal experience is available to anyone who will call out to God, according to the instructions we find in His Word.

Any person from any country on Earth who will acknowledge the Almighty God of all Creation and acknowledge His Son, the Saviour, Jesus Christ:

9. *That if thou shalt confess with thy mouth the
Lord Jesus, and shalt believe in thine heart that
God hath raised him from the dead, thou shalt be
saved.*
10. *For with the heart man believeth unto righ-
teousness; and with the mouth confession is made
unto salvation.*

— Romans 10:9–10

Yes, we need to repent.

Yes, we need to get baptized.

Next making a circumspect and patient call to God will result in this identical experience.

Am I certain this is for everyone?

Peter the apostle got sent by God to preach to the house of Cornelius — he was a Roman, a *"Gentile"* — he was not an Israelite.

What happened there gets described in great detail in the book of Acts chapters 10 and 11. Please find time to read those.

In Acts chapter 10, the result of Peter's preaching:

> 44. *While Peter yet spake these words, the Holy Ghost fell on all them which heard the word.*
> — Acts 10:44

How did they know that this remarkable miracle had happened? They heard the tangible evidence:

> 45. *And they of the circumcision which believed were astonished, as many as came with Peter, because that on the Gentiles also was poured out the gift of the Holy Ghost.*
> 46. *For they heard them speak with tongues, and magnify God. Then answered Peter,*
> 47. *Can any man forbid water, that these should not be baptized, which have received the Holy Ghost as well as we?*
> — Acts 10:45–47

When people receive the gift of the Holy Ghost they will have the same experience that I had.

It's always accompanied by *"speaking with other unlearned tongues."*

This is an unmistakable gift from God. You can not fake it. God provides the words for us to speak to Him.

I praise God for His ever merciful grace and His wonderful plan of salvation offered to all.

Chapter 5

Walk By Faith

I met Heather a few months later. For me I had the feeling of *"Love at first sight."* She was sitting a little way further along in the same row of seats and we soon got talking after the meeting.

I went home *"knowing"* that I had met the lady I was going to marry!

We started going out for dinner and going to Young People's (Youth Group) meetings and before long I had asked for her hand in marriage. I am glad she said *"Yes."*

I took Heather across to Adelaide to meet my parents and we got married the following year.

We started our married life living in a rented flat in South Yarra. Before long we decided we could live more cheaply in Kew. We moved into a more spacious flat not far from the Kew Junction.

The apartment in which we lived was close to where the church hall location was in those days.

After a while it dawned on us that although we lived so close we were often among the last to walk through the doors and find a seat. Not the best we could achieve.

Once we realised this we smartened up our game.

We decided it would be better to make sure we arrived before the opening prayer and chorus start time.

We started leaving home at least 30 minutes before we needed to. This meant we were almost never late again.

The most wonderful thing about this change was that it meant we were arriving at the church hall with enough time to meet lots of people we had not known well before and we got to chat around and hear some wonderful testimonies of God's grace and abundant blessing in their lives.

Chest Pain

While we were living in Kew a worrisome event took place. One day, after lunch I think, I experienced an angina attack. Not that we recognised it as such at the time.

I experienced what felt like a tight band around my chest.

Heather prayed for me and the pain subsided — went away.

We gave praises to God and thought no more about it, not realising what this was until years later when some heart trauma scarring showed up on a cardiogram heart scan.

This caused my medical doctor to ask *"When did you have your heart attack?"* I described this tight chest attack and recalled how we had prayed and that it had subsided after that.

In a stern voice the doctor issued his warning: *"If ever that happens again, call for an ambulance first, and then pray, by all means!"*

A House Of Our Own

We worked hard, saved a deposit for a block of land, paid that off, and then managed to get a bank loan to build our own house.

Finalising the loan application with the bank got resolved by finance regulations research followed by sincere prayer before Heather confronted the bank manager with information suggesting I had an entitlement to a *"Defence Service"* home loan because I had served in the R.A.A.F.

This meant our bank was *"obliged"* to offer us one and then provide their loan as a second mortgage behind that.

The bank branch learned something they did not know before, and we gave extensive thanks and praise to God for His all encompassing provision in our lives.

This investment required more hard work to keep paying the bank, but does appear to have been worth the effort.

Lower Back Pain

Not long after we had moved into our new house, I experienced severe pain in my lower back.

I was beginning to carry too much excess body weight.

One day the pain was so excruciating I needed to get carried in to a local Chiropractor.

With the help of some brothers and sisters from church, who first conveyed me and carried me in for pain relief, and then with the Chiropractor doing his best, while we and our dear friends were praying for me, I soon managed to walk out on my own two feet.

Thank you Lord for creating us with a body of such wonder-

ful design and thank you for the dedicated medical specialists.

Holiday Plans Can Change

Driving up to Evans Head in NSW, to attend a church
Christmas camp, we first attempted to drive East via Gipps-
land across to the coastal highway.

We had planned a leisurely drive all the way up the NSW
coast. We got as far as Morwell and our V.W. Kombi-van's
motor blew up.

Heather's brother, Keith, hired an enormous trailer and drove
all the way out (about 150 kilometres) to find us. He towed
our car, on the trailer, back to Melbourne where a wonderful brother at church, Eric Cornwall, an experienced motor
mechanic, managed to find and install a replacement short
motor for us.

We had lost about five days of travel time.

Undeterred we next headed North out of town intending to
drive up the shorter inland Newell Highway.

We got close to a town called Wallan when the motor
electrics shorted and the car would go no further.

This time, Heather's younger brother, Graeme, came out and
towed our car back to a local mechanic near our home where
we managed to get the electrical wiring repaired.

These verses came to mind:

> 1. *Therefore being justified by faith, we have peace
> with God through our Lord Jesus Christ:*
> 2. *By whom also we have access by faith into this
> grace wherein we stand, and rejoice in hope of the
> glory of God.*

*3. And not only so, but we glory in tribulations
also: knowing that tribulation worketh patience;
4. And patience, experience; and experience, hope:
5. And hope maketh not ashamed; because the love
of God is shed abroad in our hearts by the Holy
Ghost which is given unto us.*
— Romans 5:1–5

Christmas day intervened and we were most graciously invited and greatful to partake of a wonderful festive feast with a large family at church.

On Boxing Day we set off again and this time we managed to get up to Holbrook in NSW when a passing motor vehicle flicked up a stone and our windscreen got smashed!

We looked at each other and started laughing. We mightily praised our God, reminding ourselves that we knew and thoroughly believed this:

*28. All things work together for good to them that
love God, to them who are the called according to
his purpose.*
— Romans 8:28

We pushed out the broken glass from the space where the windscreen used to be and drove back over a hill where we saw a billboard advertising a windscreen repair shop! We gave them a call and soon had the windscreen replaced.

After a brief wait we continued on and completed the drive up to the Christmas camp, arriving in time for the opening chorus meeting!

Despite all those setbacks we got to hear wonderful and uplifting testimonies and Bible talks and we had one of the best times ever.

One of our favourite Bible verses is:

4. *Rejoice in the Lord alway: and again I say, Rejoice.*
— Philippians 4:4

Hang Glider Accident

Heather took up hang-gliding. She went out and took special instruction classes to learn how to partake with safety in this extreme sport. She spent hours sitting on hillsides and sand dunes waiting for suitable wind conditions and learned how to fly.

After some time Heather purchased her own hang-glider. This was a sleek new model that proved to be considerably more efficient at lift-offs than the older training craft.

Heather soon had a hang-glider accident. The craft lifted off with no effort in the breeze and in trying to correct and control her flight Heather was unable to adjust her grip on the A-frame to enable her to get sufficient control to stall the glider on landing and the A-frame hit the ground first — instead of landing on her feet.

The abrupt landing broke Heather's upper-arm in two places — a complex break with bone fragments. Her brother Graeme drove her to the nearest hospital where her broken arm got re-set in a plaster cast.

After weeks of painful recovery time where she needed to sit up all the time to allow the arm to hang down from her shoulder she found that her arm had a permanent bend.

Despite this awkward arm restriction she was happy that God had answered her prayers and had restored a considerable degree of dexterity.

World Travels

Some years later we realised we both had long-service leave. We took our leave on half pay and travelled around to different parts of the world for a total of seventeen (17) weeks.

We flew from one major destination to the next, travelling in one direction (basically Westward), and utilised other modes of transport to get around on the ground.

We travelled by aeroplane visiting Athens in Greece, Rome and Florence in Italy, Amsterdam in the Netherlands and then flew on to the UK.

We bought a second-hand Bedford *"camper-van"* in London and drove down to the ferry to cross the channel into France and continued our Europe travels.

France, Luxembourg, Belgium, Netherlands, Germany, Switzerland, Northern Italy, back to the Swiss-French border, then a rapid transit through France and we then caught the ferry back to the UK.

After a little time there we flew on to the USA (East), visited Canada, USA (West), Hawaii, Singapore, and then back home!

We had exciting and intriguing moments in those travels, and we praise our mighty God for His wonderful creation of the Earth and its peoples and for His gracious hand of guidance and protection.

I almost wiped us out in a road accident when it came to my turn to drive in Switzerland. I looked the wrong way when pulling out from a Tee intersection and turned onto the wrong side of the road. There was an enormous screech of brakes as a truck managed to come to a halt less than one metre away!

We praised God greatly for His extensive care at that time.

Later, over in the USA and Canada we used Greyhound buses and occasional hire cars to traverse some sections we wanted to spend more time exploring.

We managed to visit with members of Spirit-filled groups of our church centres in Italy, Germany, the U.K. and over in Canada. Delightful.

More Abundantly

Soon we had again driven up to Evan's Head for another Christmas camp. On the second day during the morning chorus session, Heather touched my hand and said: *"My arm!"* *"My arm!"* *"My arm!"*

I thought she must be in pain again and started to pray. I was asking God to help ease that. *"No."* she said, *"It feels all molten inside!"*

With a great beaming smile on her face she proceeded to fully extend and straighten out her arm with no visible bend. That is something she had been unable to do since the Hang Glider accident a year or two earlier.

Heather gives the Lord all the glory for that healing and one of her favourite passages of scripture is surely:

> 20. *Now unto him that is able to do exceeding abundantly above all that we ask or think, according to the power that worketh in us,*
> 21. *Unto him be glory in the church by Christ Jesus throughout all ages, world without end. Amen.*
> — Ephesians 3:20,21

Chapter 6

Long-lasting Provision

In the lead-up to the year 2000 there was an abundance of work in the I.T. field — working in teams who were trying to locate and repair instances of the Y2K bug.

The Y2K bug found its way into computer software because people were not aware that the year 2000 *was* a leap year.

Most people know every fourth year is a leap year — has 29 days in February. That is a general rule.

There is another rule that declares — if a year number is also *exactly* divisible by 100, then the year is *not* a leap year.

The year 1900 was *not* a leap year and most people thought the year 2000 would also *not* be a leap year.

A closer inspection of the rules for determining leap years in the Gregorian calendar shows there is *another* rule which says — if the year number is *exactly* divisible by 400 then the year *is* a leap year!

This is the exception that most software designers, functional and technical specifications experts, testing teams and computer programmers had missed.

I can assure you that we *did* find and fix hundreds of such instances of the Y2K bug. It was not a waste of effort. Not where I worked.

Soon, for months and months companies divested themselves of their over-staffed I.T. sections.

In 2004, I and countless others found ourselves out of work. I applied for dozens and dozens of jobs.

We found there to be a reducing number of opportunities available, and an increasing number of applicants, each vying for the same shrinking number of positions.

Almost out of the blue I stumbled across an advertisement for some work at BoM — the Bureau of Meteorology. The closing date for the application was one day away.

It would take me longer than that to get the application mailed to them, let alone the time required to compose my application with care to address their selection criteria.

There was a telephone contact number which I called and I got assured that if I got my application to them by the close of business on the Friday of that week, then they would certainly consider my application because I had taken the trouble to make that contact.

Wow! Thank you Lord, once again. I spent the next day and a bit putting together my application and then hand delivered this before 4 p.m. on that Friday with perhaps an hour or so to spare.

I waited with patience. I heard nothing for four or five weeks.

I read and re-read the advertisement. It did not promise any time frame for a response.

During this time I re-evaluated the nominal salary and I realised that even if I did manage to get the position I would be looking at a 40% pay cut from what I had been earning. Was this what I wanted?

Finances were beginning to get desperate. All the time, Heather and I were praying and believing that our wonderful God has everything in His hands.

After another two weeks I telephoned the BoM contact number again and got informed that the reason there had been a delay was that the organisation was finalising the process of moving into their new premises near the Southern Cross railway station in Collins Street on the edge of the city of Melbourne.

Hopefully the successful applicants would get notified soon if they got selected to attend for an interview.

Another week or so later I did receive a letter inviting me to go in for an interview for this position. Thank you Lord.

On the appointed day I travelled into the city, found their new offices and got escorted from Reception to a small meeting room containing three personnel who were the interview panel for the position for which I had applied.

They explained how they had made the enormous move, packing up all their office equipment, the entire computer centre and the research library from their previous old building and had migrated across into their brand new, more spacious premises.

The interview, I thought, proceeded reasonably well. They informed me that they would be making their decision later in the week and the applicants should hear about that the following week.

Sure enough, within that week a letter arrived, offering me the position. I accepted, and commenced work at 9 a.m. on the following Wednesday, 25–August–2004.

I got shown into a large corner office that I was to share with a part-time semi-retired scientist who came in one or two days each week. I had landed in my own slice of heaven.

As advertised, the position was *"non-ongoing"* and got specified for between 12 to 18 months.

On the good side, it did include a cumulative sick leave provision, and would contribute to my superannuation savings.

My salary started mid-way through a particular pay scale and there were a couple of automatic increments for the first two completed years.

Soon after this my position got extended for an unspecified period on an *"As Required"* basis.

Later, in 2011, I got promoted to a permanent position with my salary reaching close to what it had been about ten years earlier in the Y2K days.

The complex work I was doing was most enjoyable and I got made to feel that I was an integral part and an appreciated member of a highly regarded and world class Climate Science Research team.

God knew what would be good for me.

Chapter 7

God Knows Our Future

Now God knows the end from the beginning, and certainly knows our need well before we do.

These words from Isaiah come to mind:

> 9. *Remember the former things of old: for I am God, and there is none else; I am God, and there is none like me,*
> 10. *Declaring the end from the beginning, and from ancient times the things that are not yet done, saying, My counsel shall stand, and I will do all my pleasure:*
> — Isaiah 46:9–10

In October 2013, I experienced an Ischaemic Stroke episode. One day at work I began feeling awful, not right. I felt so bad that I apologised and informed my supervisor I was feeling unwell and I was leaving to take myself home.

My supervisor offered to call an ambulance for me. I stubbornly refused.

I caught the next available train and about an hour later walked through the front door at home and called out to

Heather to let her know that I was feeling unwell and was going straight to bed.

I slept all day and awoke the next morning. When I tried to get up I found that my left leg was not co-operating with my intentioned will to move it.

Heather took me to our G.P. We prayed all the way there and he ordered that I get to hospital because he thought I was having a stroke.

Heather drove me straight to the Emergency department of the hospital and I got admitted into a hospital bed and a series of tests and imaging scans got performed to help determine what was happening.

A Stroke specialist confirmed that I was experiencing an Ischaemic Stroke and this got caused by a blockage in an artery on the right-hand side of my head at the base of my brain. A part of the brain that helps to control movement on the left side of the body.

I spent another day or two in hospital and then got transferred (by ambulance) to a special rehabilitation hospital.

Soon after arrival another extensive raft of tests and scans got performed to check and cross-check the findings of the Stroke Ward from which I had come.

At that time I was unable to lift or move either my left arm or my left leg. I had impaired speech and my brain felt like a *"fuzz ball."*

It got determined that because I did not allow my supervisor to call an ambulance for me, without delay, there had been an extensive time through my travels home and my stubborn waiting overnight.

This delay caused considerable brain damage to occur — brain cells got starved of oxygen and these had *"died."*

If you ever think you or another person near you could be experiencing a stroke, there is four simple tell-tale STROKE signs. These can get remembered through the use of the first four (4) letters in the word: '*STROKE*':

1. **S** is for SMILE with ease.

   Can the person make a nice smile?

2. **T** is for TALK in clear words.

   Can the person say *"Chicken Soup?"*

3. **R** is for RAISE the arms.

   Can they raise both arms above their head.

4. **O** is for OUT with the tongue.

   Can the person poke out their tongue?
   — STRAIGHT OUT ?

   You do not want to see it lolling off
   to one side of their mouth.

These should all be *easy* tasks to do.
If ANY of those actions is awkward, please
— Call Emergency — NOW.

The next two letters can be helpful, too:

1. **K** is for KID. Do not KID yourself.

   Is ANY of those movements awkward?

2. **E** is for EMERGENCY. Call EMERGENCY — NOW.

   DO NOT WAIT, do this NOW.
   The sooner the patient gets to hospital,
   the more chance they have to get helped.

At length, Heather got permitted to visit me in my room at the rehabilitation hospital.

We got told to expect that I would need to remain at the rehabilitation facility for at least six (6) months, and they expected the best I would manage was to get allowed home in a wheel chair, or if I was able, using some form of supportive walking frame.

As we gradually digested that information, together we earnestly prayed to our God and asked for His healing power in my life.

Visiting hours were over and Heather needed to leave.

After I had eaten a small dinner and before I settled down to sleep for the night I prayed and reminded myself that *"God created all things and nothing is impossible to Him."*

We read how *"Jesus healed all those who came to Him."* I knew I could call to Him, and I knew I could expect Him to heal me.

Soon after my meditative prayer as I was lying on my bed my left leg straightened and my left foot turned in a gentle motion.

"Is that you Lord?" I asked in my mind. Again, my left leg straightened out and my left foot turned.

"I'll take that as a yes!" I said in silence to myself. Again, my left leg straightened and my left foot turned. I smiled and thanked my God for His never ending mercy.

This gentle manipulation of my left leg and foot continued. Before long I asked: *"Should I resist these actions or should I relax?"*

The leg manipulation stopped in an instant. Everything went quiet and still.

After thinking about that I realised: *"Oh! How silly. That was a double question!"*

Then I asked: *"Should I resist what You are doing?"* Still everything remained quiet.

Next I asked: *"Should I relax and let You do what You do?"* In a moment my left leg straightened and my left foot turned again. *"I'll take that as a yes,"* I concluded.

The motion of left leg straightening with the left foot turning continued to happen about a hundred times before I drifted off to a peaceful and sound sleep. I expect you've heard of *"Counting sheep?"*

The following morning I found that I had enough strength in my right arm to heave myself up on the side of the bed, and I was then able to lift myself so that I could actually stand for a moment or two before I slipped down and crumpled in a gentle heap on the floor.

Within moments the door flew open and nurses rushed in to help me back up and onto the bed again. I had triggered a motion sensor!

Later that day I started rehabilitation sessions. In physiotherapy I found that I was able to raise my left leg about five millimetres for a moment or two. That was more than I had managed to achieve for days before.

Week after week, each night, the gentle leg and foot manipulations continued. Every day I found that I was able to achieve more than I had been able to do the day before. Thank You Lord.

There were dozens of different therapy sessions. Some to explore speech, some for cognitive thinking, others for vision and eyesight and there were other sessions designed to prepare a stroke patient to help us integrate back into a new form of post-stroke life.

With each passing day I was becoming more able to move

both limbs on the left side of my body.

Soon there came a day when I could raise my left arm up over my head! My praises go to God and the caring medical staff.

I progressed from wheel chair to a high walking frame and then on to a low walking frame. Soon a pair of crutches and then managed to walk with a single walking stick.

At last, some six (6) weeks (not months) after I had arrived there I got permitted to go home for a brief visit to see if I could navigate steps and other features around our house.

Returning to the rehabilitation hospital for a final week of physiotherapy sessions I was soon permitted to return to living at home full time. Life was starting to get back to a new form of normal.

I thoroughly praise God for the healing He provided. The gradual nature of the healing process gives me more opportunity to get amazed at how wonderful is God's creation we call the human body and more of what this involves.

Please don't take it for granted and give God no thought or appreciation.

I am able to thank and praise God for every day, and for each advancement that He provides as I come to appreciate more and more about how miraculous is our design and how wonderfully are we made:

> 14. *I will praise thee; for I am fearfully and won-derfully made: marvellous are thy works; and that my soul knoweth right well.*
> — Psalms 139:14

Our God is brilliant and gracious and exceeding merciful.

At first I was unable to hold, let alone play my guitar.

Gradually, as my strength and determination returned, I have been able to do more and more.

I can now hold and play a variety of chords, and can almost strum and change chords in some semblance of rhythmic time again.

I may not be able to play all the old songs I wrote, but I have managed to compose some new pieces, and who knows where those could lead.

In 2014, I managed to get back to some part-time work. My position at the BoM was still there and for all the weeks when I was in the rehabilitation hospital the BoM granted me sick leave on full pay.

Employee recreation leave and sick leave entitlements continued to accrue over all that time.

Although I did not appreciate the full extent of God's wonderful provision when I first went to work at the BoM for a wage that was some 40% lower than what I had been earning before, I think the cumulative benefit of the weeks and weeks of sick leave on full pay far outstripped what I thought I had lost!

Once again, we praise our God for His wonderful provision.

My stroke recovery was in some ways slower than it might have been because my body was also trying to cope with a reduced blood flow of vital oxygen carrying red blood cells. I was often tired and running out of breath after little exertion.

In 2014 my G.P. sent me to a cardio specialist who performed a cardio-stress test that I failed miserably.

He determined that I could need to have a stent inserted or might need cardiac bypass surgery. More exhaustive tests determined that CABG — Coronary Artery Bypass Graft — surgery was the best option.

As a public patient there were three or four false starts. I got given probable operation times and after waiting in hospital admission wards got sent home again because there were more urgent cases like traumatic road accident emergency patients who needed to get treated ahead of me.

While I waited I managed to find a hospital staff training video all about CABG surgery and through watching this I was able to imagine how amazing are the specialists who perform such operation procedures.

A link to the CABG Surgery hospital/nursing training video I watched before I had my triple bypass is:

`https://www.YouTube.com/watch?v=t8D9BZ4BcCQ`

The video is rather long and runs for about 1 hour and 45 minutes. Certified as *"restricted"* the video contains *"graphic"* (medical) material.

This is unsuitable for young children to view and means you will need to get logged-in to Google™ or another service provider to determine your age for permission to view the content.

I watched the entire video before undergoing my CABG surgery and it helped me see that this procedure is so well understood that any risks were well worth the more probable successful outcome.

The training video demonstrated how they connect you to a Heart-Lung machine and they cool down your heart until it stops beating. This enables the team to operate on your heart to graft the necessary artery bypass segments.

Afterwards they begin a gradual warm up of the heart again and miraculously it starts to quiver and then beat again all by itself with almost no help from the operating team!

Located at points ranging from about 1 hour and 7 minutes through to 1 hour and 15 minutes is a part where the heart gets warmed-up after getting stopped for surgery and it starts to beat again.

Fascinating to see — miraculous

Before my surgery I prayed that God would help to guide the hands of those who were operating on me. Viewing this video and knowing God is able to work miracles enabled me to relax and be at peace before my operation.

In 2015 I did get into the operating theatre and underwent a successful triple bypass operation. Now I have the scars that show the extent of my open chest cavity and the places where they removed lengths of artery from my left forearm and lower right leg. I spent three or four days in hospital and felt almost no pain.

For the first hours after the operation I was in Intensive Care — soon transferred to a normal ward. Within hours of arriving there I got encouraged to get up and walk around and I remember being totally amazed that this was indeed possible so soon after the operation.

On about day three a nurse came to remove some stitches and the last small drain tube. Not long after that Heather got permitted to come in and take me back home.

There followed a series of rehabilitation sessions which combined physical exercises with educational classes designed to help us find some coping mechanisms. These were greatly appreciated.

I was still able to take the required sick leave on full pay and was able to then incorporate a part-time graduated return to work programme while my health continued to gradually improve.

I worked for two days from home at the start and then combined that with one or two days in at the office as I became more able to endure the longer days attending work each week.

In December 2018 I retired from working full time.

In 2020, during the severe Corona-virus lock-downs experienced in Victoria, a small wound on one of my toes got a bad infection. My G.P. and hospital medical specialists attempted to clear the infection through the use of different anti-biotic medicines.

After months without the desired response it got decided the best option was to amputate the offending middle toe on my left foot.

In the middle of the Covid-19 pandemic lock-downs I was able to get quick admittance to hospital for an operation to remove the toe, and again, suffered no residual pain. With the help of community nursing home visit services the foot has healed well and almost appears like I got born with a slight V-shaped foot!

Again, I praise our God for having His hand upon my life and for leading and guiding all those who care for and provide for my physical health and well-being. Our God is exceeding gracious.

I do not know how I might have coped (if at all) without the knowledge that God *is* Whom He says He is.

God is the Creator of Heaven and Earth. He is God Almighty; there's no other God beside Him.

He is God, The Heavenly Father, also manifested by His Spirit through Jesus Christ, The Lamb of God, The Perfect Sacrifice, The Saviour, and in us by the indwelling Holy Spirit.

God is Omnipotent — All Powerful, God is Omniscient — All Knowing and God is Omnipresent — Exists Everywhere at every instant in both time and space and has and will forever.

The book of Philippians reminds us that we have:

> 7. *And the peace of God, which passeth all understanding, shall keep your hearts and minds through Christ Jesus.*
> — Philippians 4:7

God provides us with a depth of comfort that knows no bounds:

> 26. *But the Comforter, which is the Holy Ghost, whom the Father will send in my name, he shall teach you all things, and bring all things to your remembrance, whatsoever I have said unto you.*
> — John 14:26

He provides for our every need in ways that show us how *"He Knows the end from the beginning."* God hears us when we call, and He will answer our every righteous prayer.

Chapter 8

Get Born Again

We know when Peter stood up to speak to the gathering crowd and in answer to the question they asked: *"What shall we do?"* he gave everyone these clear instructions:

> 38. *Then Peter said unto them, Repent, and be baptized every one of you in the name of Jesus Christ for the remission of sins, and ye shall receive the gift of the Holy Ghost.*
> 39. *For the promise is unto you, and to your children, and to all that are afar off, even as many as the LORD our God shall call.*
> — Acts 2:38–39

Repent — prepare to get your thinking changed if needed.

We might need to straighten out our lives and actions to conform to the way we know God wants us to be:

> 8. *He hath shewed thee, O man, what is good; and what doth the LORD require of thee, but to do justly, and to love mercy, and to walk humbly with thy God?*
> — Micah 6:8

From my experience, this does not hurt. Try it. We can start to feel good about ourself. Show mercy to others; do not seek revenge. Jesus says we should turn the other cheek, and forgive people who do any wrong to us.

I expect you'll find they do not know about the grace and mercy of God. Life is too short to argue.

Preach the gospel to them in a gentle manner. That could help. You could help to save another soul.

We are God's creation; not the other way around.

Don't shout at God. He can hear you.

Don't curse and swear. God will turn away.

We need to approach God in a circumspect manner with heart felt honesty and humility; a state of repentance where we want to find the truth.

We need to believe what Jesus plainly tells us:

"Ye must be born again."

It's a three step process:

1. **Repent**

   Turn aside from doing your own thing all the time.

   Make a humble and honest approach towards God.

2. **Get baptized**

   Do what God has asked us to do.

   Go through the short process of water baptism.

   It demonstrates our intentions are good.

   It takes a little bit of humility. Yes you'll get wet.

   In the church I attend we use warm water.

We have a fresh supply of shorts and tee shirts
and dry towels — for people who don't bring those.

The Bible says *"all have sinned and come short of the
glory of God.'*

Jesus died to wash away our sins.

3. **Receive God's Holy Spirit**

Ask God for the promise of the Father.

Spend time talking to God with humility and sincerity.

Worship God. Saying the word *"Hallelujah"* gives
praise to God and helps to keep us talking.

Say thank you for what you are expecting to receive.

We need to be speaking to let God change the words.

We will know the moment we receive the *"promise of
the Father"* because we will start speaking in an unlearned tongue.

If this takes a little while, do not get discouraged.
There can be issues we could need to sort out in our
mind and understanding or in our approach toward
God. I know there was for me.

Ask and keep on asking. Jesus says this:

> 7. *Ask, and it shall be given you; seek, and ye
> shall find; knock, and it shall be opened unto
> you:*
> 8. *For every one that asketh receiveth; and he
> that seeketh findeth; and to him that knocketh
> it shall be opened.*
> — Matthew 7:7–8

Before long we expect there will be a pleasant surprise:

> 7. *Wherefore (as the Holy Ghost saith, To
> day if ye will hear his voice,*
> — Hebrews 3:7

Thank You God

Dear Heavenly Father God,

The marvelous wonders of Your Creation continually over-whelms my senses encouraging my attempted admiration and appreciation of Your boundless ability.

Using my own words I am unable to realise how to begin to thank You in an appropriate way for making me a part of Your great creative handiwork.

Thank You for giving us the gift of the Holy Spirit, en-abling us to speak to You in other tongues which we have not learned.

I treasure the knowledge that the sounds and words we can so speak are entirely those You most want to hear. I praise You and worship You with those unknown words.

From the most miniscule of sub-atomic particles through to the vastness of the space-time continuum we call our known universe — Your creative genius shouts great volumes at ev-ery location. Your Word declares:

> 26. *Lift up your eyes on high, and behold who hath created these things, that bringeth out their host by number: he calleth them all by names by the greatness of his might: for that he is strong in power; not one faileth.*
> — Isaiah 40:26

As we ponder the chemical construction of the substances and materials we use to build our shelter, make our utensils and grow our food — using the bountiful supply of all that You provide — all too infrequently do we ever remember to praise You for everything You do for us in Your creation and perfection and completion.

Your Creation includes its life-giving waters and the soils in which plants can grow and flourish. They take energy from the intensity of the sunlight that You provide in just the right amounts every day.

You give us air to breathe into our lungs to refresh the content of oxygen in the blood that courses through our arteries and back through our veins to supply our vital organs with the ability to assimilate the nutrients You have placed in all the foods You provide for us to eat.

Without Your magnificent provision we would die.

When we turn our thoughts to pondering Our Creator we find God's Word to help and guide us through and we find records of miracles performed by You and Your Son Jesus Christ for anyone who will ask.

We read how nothing is impossible for Our God.

This text is not even a fraction of a fraction of a tiny skerrick of what I imagine I want to write. I find myself surrounded by my own total inadequacy to express the feelings of joy that daily flood my soul.

Then I use Your gift of the Holy Spirit, enabling me to speak to You again in other tongues.

It's comforting to know that the sounds and words you give us to speak are those we need to say and those You most want to hear because they speak our inner-most feelings — from the heart.

Thank You for everything. We look forward to the rest of

eternity where we can learn more and more about You and all Your wondrous ways.

Thank You for making a way where we can get reconciled with You.

We praise You and worship You and Your Son Jesus Christ.

Thank You for giving us the unlearned words to use.

All my love,

Lawson

Praise in Music

In my younger days I played guitar and sang in a small band at the church I have attended for almost 50 years.

This church has centres located across the world in Australia, New Zealand, Fiji, Papua New Guinea, England, Poland, Italy, Canada, the U.S.A. and in Kenya, Tanzania and Malawi in Africa and more — all *"born again"* people.

You can find out more details at its Internet link:

```
https://www.revivalcentres.org
```

We got to perform our gospel songs as occasional items on Sundays and at our Youth Group concerts and the like. We had a lot of fun and great fellowship.

Age and health issues have now slowed me down.

We made rough recordings of the music over the years and there are some examples of my music on-line.

Here is a link provided for me by YouTube:

```
https://www.youtube.com/channel/UCGJLkNlYynw3g5_wP141S2w
```

Note: You can find sixteen (16) different songs. Each YouTube *track* has a single *still* image, not a video clip — other than the advertising they seem to display — please hit

"Skip" when that appears after about five seconds. Each music track should be playable on a low bandwidth connection and will not use too much of your Internet data limit.

A web browser search may need to use quotation marks around my two names because there is other people called *"Lawson,"* and a band named *"Hanson,"* none of whom is the same *"Lawson Hanson"* who resides in my skin.

You should find a *"Remixed: Lord God Almighty,"* and other songs like: *"Faith,"* *"He Is Lord,"* *"On A Day Like This"* and *"Prodigal Son."*

Otherwise, there are two *Albums,* each of which has eight tracks. I distributed those through DistroKid™and people should be able to find the tracks through digital download and/or audio streaming services like: Amazon™, Apple Music™, Spotify™and others.

An example of these located at Apple Music is:

- He Is Lord

  https://music.apple.com/au/album/he-is-lord/1473958665

- Prodigal Son's Return

  https://music.apple.com/au/album/prodigal-sons-return/1473966231

Or on Spotify:

- He Is Lord

  https://open.spotify.com/album/6TC5awGoyok3cXY7fU9tkl

- Prodigal Son's Return

  https://open.spotify.com/album/5RuDTHcTKAzYYoKHBeO50s

Accreditations

Over the course of more than four decades I have performed my music live with the accompaniment of different musicians.

I offer my sincere thanks and great appreciation to the talented individuals who spent countless hours of their precious time in rehearsals and preparations for the performances we managed to present.

Accompanying my own lyrics, melodies, vocals and rhythm guitar, the recordings variously include other instrumental and vocal performances by these people:

By Musical Instrument

- Bass Guitar:

    - Bradley Parker-Hill
    - Mark Stanborough

- Drums:

    - Jonathon Longfield
    - Mark Stanborough
    - Nigel Picknell
    - Paul Anastassopoulos
    - Stuart Bowden

- Lead Guitar:

    - Clive Smith
    - Mark Stanborough

- Saxophone:

    - Mark Stanborough

- Peter deMunk

- Sound Recording:
  - Mark Stanborough
- Vocals:
  - Paul Anastassopoulos
  - Peter deMunk

By the same author

Nonfiction

Epub

Love, Joy, Peace
Living a better life by the Grace of God
2025, ISBN 9791764057844

.

Glory to God Everywhere You Are There
Describes the origins of my simple song of praise
2025, ISBN 9781764057820

.

Jesus Says You Must Be Born Again
The most important information the world affords
2025, ISBN 9781764057813

Nonfiction

Paperback

Love, Joy, Peace
Living a better life by the Grace of God
2025, ISBN 9791764057851

.

Glory to God Everywhere You Are There
Describes the origins of my simple song of praise
2025, ISBN 9781764057837

.

Jesus Says You Must Be Born Again
The most important information the world affords
2025, ISBN 9781764057806

.

Paul's Question
Have you received the Holy Spirit?
2023, ISBN 9798857128381

.

Linux Bread Crumbs
Learn to use Linux
2023, ISBN 9798364005830

.

To Day If You Will Hear His Voice
Believe in God
2022, ISBN 9798831130669

.

Take Another Look
Please take another look
2022, ISBN 9798437605554

.

Song Lyrics
Notes and lyrics for 16 of my songs
2022, ISBN 9798434494120

Fiction

Paperback

The Ravenscroft Algorithm
Fictitious cyber crime
2022, ISBN 9798842106202

Broke Reef
Fictitious shipwreck on a W.Aust. Reef

www.ingramcontent.com/pod-product-compliance
Lightning Source LLC
Chambersburg PA
CBHW060536030426
42337CB00021B/4290